TITLE II-A

GAMES

(and how
to
play them)

pictures by Anne Rockwell

THOMAS Y. CROWELL COMPANY, NEW YORK

For Hannah, Elizabeth & Oliver

Library of Congress Cataloging in Publication Data
Rockwell, Anne F
    Games (and how to play them)
      SUMMARY: Instructions for forty-three games
including "Simon Says," "Pussy Wants a Corner,"
and "Prisoner's Base."
      1. Games—Juvenile literature.   [1. Games]
I. Title.
GV1203.R574   793.4   72-10936
ISBN 0-690-32159-7
ISBN 0-690-32160-0 (lib. bdg.)

Manufactured in the United States of America

ISBN 0-690-32159-7

0-690-32160-0 (LB)

1 2 3 4 5 6 7 8 9 10

CONTENTS

ON YOUR MARK, GET SET, GO!

91422

PUSH PIGGY TO MARKET

This game is for two teams.
There should be at least four players on each team.
Mark a starting line with a stick or chalk.
Ten or fifteen feet away mark a goal, or "market" line.
Give each team an empty soda bottle and a three-foot stick.
Blow a whistle or say "On your mark, get set, GO!"
At this signal the first player in line on each team starts
to roll the bottle, or "piggy" to the market line
with the stick, holding one hand behind his back at all times.
As soon as a player reaches the market line
he must turn around and push the piggy back to the starting line.
Then he gives the stick to the next player on his team.
The game is won when all of the players on one of the teams
have pushed their team's piggy to and from market.
If a player makes the piggy hop, or removes his hand from behind
his back, he must return to the starting line
and begin all over again.

1

I LOVE MY LOVE

I love my love with an **A** because she is so artistic.

I love my love with a **B** because he is so belligerent.

I love my love with a **C** because he is so cautious.

I love my love with a **D** because he is so daring.

I love my love with an **E** because she is so elegant.

I love my love with an **F** because he is so friendly.

I love my love with a **G** because she is so generous.

. . . and so on through the entire alphabet. Any number of people can play this game. All of the players sit in a circle and take turns thinking of a word. The first player who cannot think of any adjective that starts with the next letter of the alphabet is out. Some players leave out the letter "X" because there are so few words beginning with this letter. The game can be continued when "Z" is reached by starting again with "A."

CHINESE HOP

This game is for two teams of at least
five players each. The game is more fun if there
are more players to participate. Each team lays
out a row of sticks. The sticks should be
about eighteen inches apart. There must be
as many sticks in each row as there are
players on each team. As soon as the starter
blows a whistle or says "On your mark, get set,
GO!" the first player on each team hops on one
foot over every stick, picks up the last
stick in the row, and, still standing on one
foot, turns and hops back over the remaining
sticks. As soon as he returns he taps the
player who is next in line on his team.
This player then hops over all the remaining
sticks, picks up the last one, and returns.
The next player after him proceeds. Any player
whose foot touches a stick must go back to the
starting stick and start over. The same rule
holds if anyone puts both feet on the ground.
The first team to pick up all of its sticks wins.

DRAGON TAG

This game requires at least ten players.
Four players link their arms together, forming a chain.
These four players are the "dragon."
They must not let go of each other's arms,
but must always run linked together in this manner.
The dragon runs around and tries to catch as many players
at one time as it can, by forming a circle around them.
As soon as one or more of the players is circled
by the dragon he must link arms with the others on the
dragon and help to capture the remaining players.
The game is over when everyone has been tagged
and is part of one long dragon.

KING OF THE CASTLE

Any number can play this game. Choose a King by drawing straws or counting out. The King then mounts his "castle," which may be a rock, or a wooden box, or a tree stump. If none of these are available you can draw a chalk circle about three feet in diameter around the king. As soon as he mounts his castle he shouts to the other players, "I'm the King of the Castle, and you're a dirty rascal!" At this challenge all of the other players try to push or pull the King off his castle. Any player who succeeds in doing so becomes the next King and challenges all the others. However, it is against the rules to pull the King by his clothes. Anyone who does so becomes his prisoner and is out of the game.

GIANT STEPS

This game is for four or more players.
One player is chosen by drawing straws or counting out
to be the Mother. She stands about fifty feet
away from the others, who stand lined up in a row.
She calls out the name of the first player, saying, for example,
"John may take two giant steps." John answers, "Mother, may I?"
and takes two very long strides forward.
Mother then calls the name of the next player, saying, for example,
"Lisa may take ten baby steps." Lisa then says, "Mother, may I?"
and takes ten steps forward, as small as possible.
The game continues in this way with Mother calling for giant
or baby steps from each player until one player
is close enough to tag her. Then that player becomes
the new Mother, and calls the steps after all the others
have returned to the starting place. But if any player moves
forgetting to say, "Mother, may I?" he loses his turn
and must stay where he was until the next turn.

COFFEEPOT

This is a guessing game. Any number can play. One player, who is chosen by drawing straws or counting out, leaves the room while the others think of some activity, such as dancing, swimming, cooking, reading, sleeping, etc. The activity they choose is called "Coffeepot." When the absent player is called back he tries to guess what coffeepotting is by asking each player a question such as, "Do you coffeepot in the dark?" or "Can rabbits coffeepot?" until he guesses what coffeepot means. All questions must be answered truthfully with "yes" or "no." When the questioner thinks he has guessed what coffeepot is he may ask if his guess is correct, and if it is, the player who answered his last question goes out of the room and a new activity is chosen as coffeepot. But if the questioner guesses wrong three times he is out of the game.

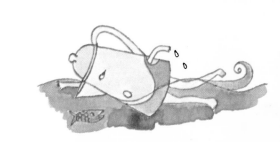

CAT AND RAT

For this game at least eight players
are needed. Six (or more) join hands
forming a circle. One player stands in
the center of the circle. He is the Rat
whom the Cat is trying to catch. One player,
who stands outside the circle, is the Cat.
Cat and Rat are chosen by counting out or
drawing straws. The Cat tries to break
through the circle and catch the Rat but
the other players try to keep him out by
raising and lowering their arms. If the
Cat breaks through and catches the Rat
the Rat is allowed to choose any other
player to be the Rat in the center, and
he becomes the Cat.

SARDINES

Any number can play.
This is a good game to play indoors
where there are plenty of hiding places such as
in closets, under tables or behind chairs and sofas.
One player is chosen by drawing straws or counting out
to be the first Sardine. The other players
leave the room and slowly count to one hundred while
the Sardine hides. Then they all begin to hunt for him.
The first one to find him hides in the same place, quickly and quietly.
The next players to find the two of them hide there too.
But when they do, they don't tell anyone else.
The game continues until everyone is hiding in the same place.
Then the person who first discovered the hiding place becomes
the next Sardine. Now he
hides and the others try to find him.
It's very hard not to make a noise or giggle
when someone finds the Sardine.

QUACK! QUACK!

Any number can play, but this game is more fun
the more players there are.
One player is chosen
by drawing straws or counting out.
He is blindfolded with a kerchief and given
a cane or a yardstick ruler or a closed umbrella.
The other players march around and around him in a circle.
As soon as he taps his cane loudly on the floor everyone stops.
The blindfolded player points his cane at someone and
that person must say "Quack! Quack!"
The blindfolded player tries to guess who it is.
If he guesses correctly the first time, he trades places
with that player, who is then blindfolded and given the cane.
But if he guesses wrong, everyone marches around him again
until he taps and points and someone says "Quack! Quack!"

HOPSCOTCH

Here is one of many ways to play hopscotch.
Draw a diagram about ten feet long like the one
in the picture. Each player must have a coin,
pebble, or bottlecap. This is a "potsie."
The first player tosses his potsie into box 1,
hops over 1 on one foot, into 2, then 3. At 4
and 5 he puts both feet down at the same time, one
into each box. Then he hops on one foot into 6, puts
both feet down, one in 7 and one in 8, jumps around
to face the other way, with feet in 7 and 8 again,
and then hops back through all the boxes until
he reaches 2. Here he bends over on one foot,
picks up his potsie, hops into 1 and out.
Then he tosses the potsie into 2, hops into 1,
over 2, and continues as before,
picking up his potsie on the way out. He then
tosses the potsie into 3 and so on through all
the boxes. If a player tosses his potsie into
the wrong box he must toss it back into the last
box he played, and stop. The next player takes
his turn. One must also stop playing, leaving
his potsie wherever it is if he puts two feet
in one box or touches a line with hand or foot.
The next player does not need to play a box with
someone else's potsie there. The first player to finish
is the winner. No more than four players should play.

FORFEITS

This is most fun with a large number of players. A judge and leader are chosen by drawing straws or counting out. The leader collects some small item such as a ribbon, or pencil, or shoelace from everyone but the judge. The leader puts them in a box.

The judge sits facing the players with his back to the leader.

The leader takes any item and holds it high over the head of the judge, saying, "Heavy, heavy hangs over your head. What shall the owner do to redeem it?" The judge then names a forfeit that the owner must pay to get his possession back, without knowing what the item is or who it belongs to. He may say, "Spell hippopotamus backward" or "Push a peanut five feet with your nose" or anything he thinks of that is silly.

READY OR NOT, HERE I COME

This game is for any number of players
greater than four. One player is chosen
by counting out or drawing straws
to be It. He hides his eyes against
a tree, or other place chosen to be Home,
and begins to count slowly to one hundred
by fives. All the others run to find a
hiding place. When It reaches one hundred
he calls out, "Ready or not, here I come!"
and hunts for the others. When he sees
someone he calls out "I spy—" and names
whomever he sees. That player then races him
Home and if he reaches there first he calls
"Home free!" but if It tags him before he is
home free he becomes It and calls out,
"Everybody home free!" Then all the others
come out of hiding. The new player who is It
then hides his eyes, counts to one hundred
by fives, and the others run and hide from him.

...25, 30, 35,
40,
45, 50...

FIZZ-BUZZ

This game is played with as many players as possible. Everyone sits in a row or circle. The first player in the row begins to count, but when the turn is reached of the player who would say "5" or any multiple of 5, he says "Fizz" instead. "Buzz" is harder. The taboo number is 7, and when 7, or any multiple of it, or any number containing 7 is reached, that player must say "Buzz." In "Fizz-Buzz" both 5 and 7 are taboo, with "Fizz" said at 5 and "Buzz" said at 7. Any player who says a taboo number instead of "Fizz" or "Buzz" is out of the game. You can play "Fizz" or "Buzz" or "Fizz-Buzz," depending on how difficult you want the game to be.

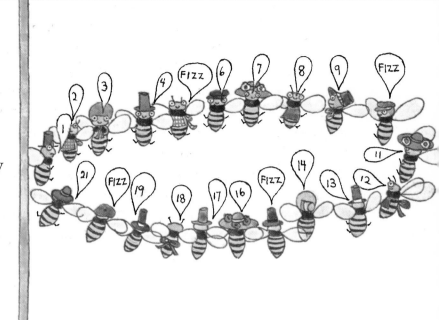

POISON

Any number can play.
A pot or kettle is placed on the ground.
Five or more players join hands, forming a circle
around the pot. One player is chosen by drawing straws or
counting out to be the leader. He tries to push
or pull the other players so that one of them knocks his foot
against the pot. As soon as any player touches the pot
he is "poison" and all the other players run away from him.
The player who is poison chases them until he catches someone.
Then that player becomes the leader.
Everyone joins hands in a circle again while the new leader
tries to make someone else touch the pot
and become poison.

LEAPFROG

Any number can play.
Players line up, one after another.
The first player in line bends his knees
and squats down, bracing his hands on
his knees. The second player in line puts
his hands on the squatting player's back,
spreads his legs wide, and leaps over
the first player. The third player leaps
over both of them, and so on, with all
players leaping and then taking the squatting
position. When all players are squatting
in a row, the last player jumps up and leaps
over all of them. The player next to him
continues, and so on. You can leapfrog
as great a distance as you like, or you may
decide beforehand on a definite distance to go.

FOR RENT
CALL
122-6672

I TOOK A TRIP

This is an alphabet game for any number of players. The players sit in a row and the first begins by saying that he took a trip to a place beginning with "A." The next player repeats his sentence and adds that he took something beginning with "B." The third adds something that begins with "C" and so on through the alphabet. However, each player must repeat everything that has been said by everyone else. Anyone who forgets a word is out.

I took a trip to Alaska.

I took a trip to Alaska with a bumblebee.

I took a trip to Alaska with a bumblebee and a cabbage.

I took a trip to Alaska with a bumblebee, a cabbage and a donkey.

I took a trip to Alaska with a bumblebee, a cabbage, a donkey and an elf.

I took a trip to Alaska with a bumblebee, a cabbage, a donkey, an elf and a flower.

I took a trip to Alaska with a bumblebee, a cabbage, a donkey, an elf, a flower, and a glockenspiel...

17

FEATHERS, FEATHERS

This game is for five or more players. A leader is chosen by drawing straws or counting out. He starts the game by saying, "Feathers, Feathers, Chicken Feathers!" and flapping his arms in a flying motion. All the other players then flap their arms. He calls out "Feathers, Feathers" again and again, usually naming some creature that has feathers, and always flapping his arms. But suddenly he may call out, "Feathers, Feathers, Pig Feathers!" or any other creature that doesn't have feathers, still flapping his arms. Anyone else, however, who flaps his arms when he names something without feathers is out of the game. The leader calls "Feathers, Feathers" as fast as he can to confuse the players and make them flap when they shouldn't.

18

PUSSY WANTS A CORNER

This is a game for five players.
It should be played indoors.
At the beginning of the game all five
players rush for the four corners
of the room. One player does not get
a corner. This player is the Pussy.
She goes to each of the players in
the corners, saying plaintively,
"Pussy wants a corner." Each player
answers in turn, "Go to my next-door
neighbor." Pussy begs for a corner
from each player; each refuses her.
She then stands in the middle
of the room and calls, "Change places!"
At this, everyone trades corners
quickly with a neighbor. During this
confusion, when the corners are vacant,
Pussy tries to steal one. The player
who loses his corner becomes Pussy.
If Pussy fails to get a corner, she must
try again.

BUTTON, BUTTON

This game is for eight or more players. One player is chosen by drawing straws or counting out to be It. All the players except the one who is It sit in a circle on the floor. It sits in the middle of the circle. The players in the circle have a button which they keep passing from hand to hand. They keep their hands in constant motion so that it looks as if they all are passing the button at the same time. The player in the center tries to guess who has the button. When he guesses correctly that person trades places with him and takes his turn guessing who has the button.

YANKEE DOODLE CRACKER

This game is for two teams
of at least four players on each team, and a referee.
The referee gives everyone a saltine cracker.
As soon as he blows a whistle, or calls, "On your mark,
get set, GO!" the first person on each team eats his cracker
and tries to whistle "Yankee Doodle went to town,
a-riding on his pony, stuck a feather in his cap and called it
macaroni!" As soon as he has succeeded in whistling
it the next player on his team eats his cracker
and tries to whistle the same tune.
This is not easy with a mouth full of cracker crumbs.
The first team to finish is the winner.

GOSSIP

This game requires at least ten players.
However, it is more fun with as many as possible.
Everyone sits or stands in a row. The first player in line
makes up a sentence composed of three parts.
The sentence must say where someone is, with whom, and what
the two of them are doing. You may say, for example,
"I saw Molly Jones on Green Mountain with little Tommy picking
dandelions." or "Miss Lizzy went to market with Jenny Jane
to buy some sweet potatoes." The person who thought of the sentence
whispers it to the person next in line, who whispers it
to the next in line, and so on to the end of the line.
The last person repeats out loud what he has heard.
It is usually very funny to hear the way the sentence
has changed its original meaning after so many people
have passed on the gossip.

KICK THE CAN

This game is for five to ten players.
One is chosen by counting out or
drawing straws to be It. A tree
is chosen as Home. It kicks
a tin can as far as he can from Home
and goes to fetch it and bring it
Home. While he is doing this
the other players run and hide.
As soon as he has returned the can,
It goes to search for the others.
As soon as he sees someone he calls,
"Tap, tap on—" and names whomever
he sees. That person then races It
Home. If It gets Home first he takes
the player prisoner. But if
the player reaches Home first
he kicks the can as far as he can.
Then It must go and fetch it and
bring it back before he can hunt for
any other players. The player who
kicked the can may hide again.
If It has taken any prisoners,
he may also free one of them to hide
again. The game is over when It
has made prisoners of everyone.

MUSICAL CHAIRS

This game is for eight or more
players. One extra person is needed
to play the piano or lift the needle
from a phonograph to start and stop
the music. Arrange a row of chairs
so that one chair faces frontwards,
the next one backwards, the next
one frontwards and so on.
There should be one less
chair than there are players.
As soon as the music starts everyone
marches around the row of chairs,
staying very close to them,
but not touching them. Without
warning, the music stops. The moment
it does, all players scramble
for a chair. The player who does not
get one must drop out of the game and one
chair is removed. The music starts
and everyone marches again. When it
stops there is another scramble for
chairs, another player drops out, and
another chair is removed. The game
continues in this way until there are
two players and one chair left.
The player who manages to seat
himself in the last chair wins.

SPUD

Any number can play this game.
The players line up and the first player
in line bounces a soft rubber ball.
As he bounces it he calls out the name
of a player and then throws the ball high in
the air. The player whose name
was called runs to get the ball while
the others scatter. After he gets
the ball, he throws it, trying to hit
one of the players as they all run
to dodge it. If he misses he has one
"spud" against him. If he manages to hit
someone that player must take his turn
trying to hit someone with the ball.
If he misses three times and has
three "spuds" against him, he must bend over
and let all the others take a turn
throwing the ball at him.

DROP THE HANDKERCHIEF

From among ten or more players one player is chosen
by counting out or drawing straws to be It. All the others
stand in a circle. It walks rapidly around the outside of
the circle, carrying a handkerchief. It surprises some player
by dropping the handkerchief behind him. As soon as that player
realizes that the handkerchief is behind him he picks it up
and runs around the circle chasing It. If It reaches
the vacant place in the circle first the other player becomes It.
If the player who had the handkerchief dropped behind him
catches It he returns to his place and It must drop the handkerchief
again. If the player never notices that It has dropped
the handkerchief behind him and It manages to go all around
the circle without being chased, then that player becomes
a Dead Fish and goes to the center of the circle. A Dead Fish
can escape by picking up the handkerchief from behind someone else
and chasing It in that player's place. If he catches It
he resumes his place in the circle. If not, he is It.

26

SIMON SAYS

The more that play the better the game will be.
Choose Simon by drawing straws or counting out.
Simon gives orders to the other players such as,
"Simon says hands on your head!" and all the players
must obey immediately. However, one must never obey him
if he does not say "Simon says" before giving the order.
Anyone who does is out. Simon tries to confuse
the players either by carrying out an order
without saying "Simon says," or by doing something
other than what he ordered. For instance,
he may say, "Simon says hands on hips,"
and he may put his hands on his shoulders instead.
The one who stays in the game the longest wins
and can be the next Simon.

This game is for two players.
One player thinks of something
he can see—a telephone, for
example. Then he says, "I spy,
with my little eye, something that
begins with 'T.'" The other player
tries to guess what it is by asking only
questions that can be answered by
"yes" or "no." When he guesses what
the thing is, it is his turn to
think of something and say, "I spy,
with my little eye, something that
begins with —." This game can also
be played with a group by having one
player leave the room while the other
players think of something for him
to guess. He then questions them
each in turn.

I SPY

HAVE YOU SEEN MY SHEEP?

This game is for ten or more players.
It is more fun with a large number.
A Shepherd is chosen by counting out or
drawing straws. All the other players
stand in a circle. The Shepherd walks
around the circle and taps one player on
the back, saying, "Have you seen my sheep?"
"What does it look like?" asks the player
and the Shepherd describes the "lost sheep."
He may say, "She is wearing a watch
and blue sneakers." and the player tries
to guess who it is. When he names
the right person the Shepherd says,
"That's my sheep!" and the other player
chases the lost sheep outside and around
the circle. If the chaser catches
the lost sheep before he can return to
his place the lost sheep becomes the
Shepherd. If the lost sheep gets there
first then the first Shepherd must
try again. The Shepherd takes the place
in the circle of whoever is the new Shepherd.

FOX AND GEESE

This is a good game to play in the snow
or on the beach. When there are five or more players
choose a Fox by drawing straws or counting
out. The rest are Geese. Trample down
a circle about twenty feet in diameter.
This makes a wheel. Then trample down
six spokes. The hub, where the spokes meet
in the center, is the goal. The Fox chases
the Geese in and out and around the paths
formed by the wheel. Geese may jump across
from one spoke to another but the Fox may not.
Only one Goose at a time is safe in the hub.
If another Goose enters, the first one is no longer safe.
Only the last Goose may not be tagged.
No player may leave the paths.
Any goose tagged by the Fox is Fox
for the next turn.

GHOST

Three or more players sit in a row and one begins by saying any letter of the alphabet. The next adds a letter. Each player must add a letter but each tries not to complete a word. (Two-letter words don't count). Any player who completes a word becomes a half-ghost and no one may speak to him. Half-ghosts can go on playing, and they try to trick the others into speaking to them. Anyone who speaks to a half-ghost, or answers one, becomes a ghost. Any half-ghost who completes a second word becomes a whole ghost. Ghosts are out of the game. The winner is the last player left.

HAWK AND HEN

...A Hawk and a Hen are chosen by counting out or drawing straws. As soon as the Hen says "Oh no, you won't!" the player chosen to be Hawk jumps up from a squatting position and begins the chase. All of the other players, who are Chickens, are lined up in a row behind the Hen, each with his hands on the shoulders of the player ahead of him. The Chickens must keep this position, no matter how fast they run. The Hawk may catch only the last Chicken in line. He can't catch Hen. The Hen tries to protect her Chickens by holding out her arms and waving them in front of the Hawk and turning and dodging him. The last Chicken to be caught is Hawk for the next turn.

KNOT CONTEST

This game is for two teams with
at least eight players on each team.
It is more fun the more players there are.
Take two long pieces of rope and tie
as many tight knots in each piece as
there are players on each team.
The first player on each team unties
the first knot, taps the person next
in line on his team, and hands him
the rope. Then that person unties
the second knot, taps the third person,
who unties the third knot, and so on.
The team that first unties all the knots
in its rope is the winner.

PRISONER'S BASE

Two teams of about ten players each mark two parallel lines
about seventy-five feet apart. Behind each line, at opposite ends,
they mark a rectangle. These are Prisons. The area
between lines is No Man's Land. Everyone lines up behind the line
of his team. One team sends a player into the middle of No Man's Land.
A player from the other team runs from behind his line
and tries to tag him. If he succeeds he puts that player in
his team's Prison. If he cannot tag him and the other player
returns to safety behind his own line, the second player may be tagged.
The rule is that a player may be tagged only if he has entered
No Man's Land before the one trying to tag him. A player cannot
be tagged while walking a Prisoner to Prison. A Prisoner may be rescued
if a member of his team gets close enough to the Prison without
being tagged. A Prisoner need only keep one foot in Prison.
If there are a number of Prisoners they can form a chain out into
No Man's Land. Only the last Prisoner keeps his foot in Prison
but only the first Prisoner in line may be rescued.
The rescuer cannot be tagged while taking the Prisoner back to their base.
The team capturing the most Prisoners wins.

BEAST, BIRD, FISH

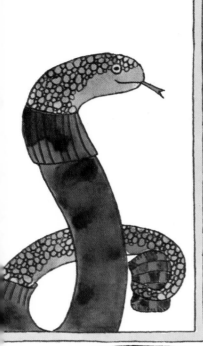

This game is for eight or more players. Everyone sits in a circle. One player is chosen by counting out or drawing straws to be It. He is given a beanbag. He tosses the beanbag to anyone in the circle, calling out the words, "Beast, Bird, Fish, *Fish!*" and the person who caught the beanbag must name some kind of fish, before It counts to ten. If It calls "Beast, Bird, Fish, *Bird!*" the person catching the beanbag must name some kind of bird, and if he says "Beast, Bird, Fish, *Beast!*" the player must name a kind of beast. If whoever catches the beanbag cannot name anything by the time It counts to ten, or if he names something that has already been named, he trades places with the player in the center and becomes It.

BEAST, BIRD, FISH! FISH!

COD.

BEAST, BIRD, FISH! BIRD!

ROBIN.

BEAST, BIRD, FISH! BEAST!

CAT!

CROWS AND CRANES

This is a game for two teams with at least
eight players on each team. One team is called Crows and
the other Cranes. A caller is chosen by drawing straws or
counting out. Each team draws a goal line about one hundred feet
from the other. Both teams line up behind their goal lines.
The caller stands in the middle of the playing area,
between both goal lines. When he calls, "Start walking!"
both Crows and Cranes walk slowly toward him. When they are
quite close to him, he calls out "Cr-r-r-r-r-ows!"
or "Cr-r-r-r-r-anes!" and whichever team he names starts to run
for its goal line. The other team chases them and tries to tag
as many players as possible before they are safe
behind their own goal line. The tagged players join the
opposing team, and both teams return to their goal lines
and the caller calls again. The game is won by the team that tags
the most players. The caller tries to keep the teams
guessing which he will call by dragging out the "Cr-r-r-r" sound
as long as possible.

STATUE TAG

This is a game for about ten players.
One player is chosen by counting out or
drawing straws to be It. Mark a starting
line with a stick or chalk. It stands
fifty feet away from this line with his back
to the other players. He counts to ten
and everyone starts to walk or run toward him.
As soon as he reaches ten he turns around
quickly and all the players must "turn to
statues." This means that they must stay
in exactly the positions they were in when
he said ten. Anyone caught moving,
even a tiny bit, is sent back to the starting
line by It. Then It counts to ten again.
As soon as any player is close enough to tag
It, he does so, and all the other players
run back toward the starting line with It
chasing them. If a player is tagged by It,
he becomes It for the next turn.

OCEAN WAVE

This game is for ten or more players.
Each one sits in a chair. The chairs are arranged in a circle.
One player goes to the middle of the circle, leaving his chair
empty. He then calls "Slide right!" or "Slide left!"
and all players move quickly into the chair to the right
or left of them. There is always an empty seat which the player
in the middle tries to grab. He may keep changing the direction
he calls and the constant motion of shifting players
looks like an ocean wave. When the player in the center
finally grabs a chair the player who should have taken that chair
becomes It. Then he goes to the center
and calls the direction. If It had just called "Slide right!"
for example, the player to the left of the empty chair
becomes It, and if he had just called "Slide left!"
the player to the right of the empty chair becomes It.

SLIDE LEFT!

38

RED ROVER, RED ROVER

This game is for two teams with at least six players on each team. The players hold hands very tightly with their teammates and form a line, facing the other team, with about fifty feet between them. One team calls out, "Red Rover, Red Rover, let —— come over!" and they name anyone they wish from the opposing team. That player runs toward them and tries to break through the clasped hands of two of the players. If he succeeds he returns to his own team. But if he fails he joins hands with one of the players on either end of the opposing team. Each team takes turns calling "Red Rover, Red Rover . . ." and the game is won by the team that succeeds in taking the most players from the opposing team.

RED ROVER,
RED ROVER,
LET
WILLIAM COME
OVER!

HAVE YOU SEEN MY FLUTE?

This is a nonsense game. Five or more players sit in a row. The first player says to the one on his right, "Have you seen my flute?" and the second player asks, "Does it toot?" First player says, "It toots" and second player asks, "How does it toot?" "Tweedle-weedle-toot!" says first player. Then second player turns to third player, saying, "Have you seen his flute?" Third player says, "Does it toot?" to first player, who answers, "It toots." "How does it toot?" asks third player and first player says "Tweedle-weedle-toot!" Third player then asks fourth player who comes back to first player, and so on. Anyone who gets mixed up and makes a mistake trades places with first player and toots like a flute.

LAME WOLF

This game is for six or more players.
One player is chosen by drawing straws or
counting out to be the Lame Wolf. All of
the other players are Lambs. Draw a box
or circle on the ground with a stick or chalk.
This is the Wolf's Den. Draw another about
fifty feet away. This is the Lamb's Pen.
Lame Wolf stands inside his Den and the Lambs
run up close to him and taunt him by saying,
"Lame Wolf, tame wolf, can't catch me!"
Then they run away. Lame Wolf tries to catch
them, but he may only run three steps before
he must hop on one foot to capture Lambs.
Any lamb who is caught by the Lame Wolf becomes
a Lame Wolf too and must help capture any
remaining Lambs. When a Lamb is caught
the others go back to their Pen and the
Lame Wolves go back to their Den. Then the Lambs
come out and taunt the Lame Wolves again.
The last Lamb to be caught is the winner.

41

BULL IN THE RING

This game is for eight or more players.
One player is chosen to be the bull
by drawing straws or counting out. Everyone
except the bull joins hands to form a ring,
with the bull in the center. The bull tries
to break out of the ring by dashing and
lunging against their joined hands. Everyone
in the ring must hold hands very tightly
to keep the bull in the ring. He is not allowed
to go under or over their arms. If the bull
breaks out of the ring he runs away and
the other players chase and try to tag him.
The one who tags him becomes the bull and a
new ring is formed from which he must try
to escape.

HUL GUL

This game is for two players.
Each player has ten dried beans, buttons, or pebbles.
One player puts as many of his beans as he likes in his fist
and holds it out to the other player, saying, "Hul Gul."
The other player replies, "Handful" and the one holding the fist
says, "How many?" At this time, the other player makes a guess
as to how many beans are in the fist. If he guesses more than
there are, he must give the other player as many beans
as are needed to make up the difference.
But if he guesses fewer beans than there are,
the other player must give him the difference.
If he guesses exactly right, he takes the whole fistful.
They take turns holding out fists and guessing.
The game is won when one player has won all the other's beans
or until they decide to stop. In that case, each player
counts his beans and the one with the most wins.

About Anne Rockwell

Asked how she decided to do a book about children's games, Anne Rockwell says, "It was the traditional nature of the subject, plus my own nostalgia for the games I had played (especially as I watched my own children and their friends playing the same games)...and the pictorial possibilities were freer, and wilder and gayer than any books I had previously done."

In each of the lovingly detailed watercolor illustrations in this book Anne Rockwell has incorporated a wealth of references to literary and artistic sources of inspiration, as well as interpreting the essence of each game itself in lively animal caricatures.

Anne Rockwell is the well-known author and illustrator of many children's books including *Munachar & Manachar, The Dancing Stars,* and *The Wolf Who Had a Wonderful Dream.* Born in Tennessee, she spent much of her childhood in New Mexico and Arizona. Later, coming to New York, she studied at the Pratt Graphic Arts Center and the Sculpture Center, but is largely a self-taught artist, and says that she cannot remember a time when she was not both drawing and writing. She and her husband, who is also an artist, have three children. The Rockwells love to travel, but now call Old Greenwich, Connecticut, home.